VIETNAMESE

Colophon

© 2003 Rebo International b.v., Lisse, The Netherlands

www.rebo-publishers.com – info@rebo-publishers.com

This 2nd edition reprinted 2004

Original recipes and photographs: © R&R Publishing Pty. Ltd.

Design, editing and production: Minkowsky Graphics, Enkhuizen, The Netherlands

Translation and adaptation: American Pie, London, UK and Sunnyvale, California, USA

ISBN 90 366 1484 8

VIETNAMESE

discover light, inspiring cookery from Vietnam for
creative cooking

REBO
PUBLISHERS

Foreword

Vietnamese cuisine is characterized by an abundance of fresh ingredients –
fragrant spices, vegetables, and fruits. Dairy products are rarely used and sauces
are not thickened with cornstarch as frequently as in Chinese cooking. Fat is used
sparingly and, in contrast to the neighboring countries, not all dishes are highly
seasoned. Favorite cooking methods are steaming,grilling, broiling, or sautéing,
the best ways to preserve the nutrients. Most dishes contain fish, crustaceans,
or mollusks. This book will reveal a cuisine consisting of healthy and easily
digestible food that also indulges your senses. There are so many delightful
and mouth-watering dishes to be discovered, ranging from Soup with Cabbage
Packages to Noodle Pancake with Garlic Beef and Turkey with Mushrooms. Happy
cooking!

Abbreviations

tbsp = tablespoon

tsp = teaspoon

g = gram

kg = kilogram

fl oz = fluid ounce

lb = pound

oz = ounce

ml = milliliter

l = liter

°C = degree Celsius

°F = degree Fahrenheit

Where three measurements are given,

the first is the American cup measure.

Method

1. If white asparagus is unavailable, use frozen or fresh asparagus (in this case, add the fresh asparagus to the broth from the very beginning and cook until tender, before adding the remaining ingredients).

2. Combine the broth, 1 tbsp/15ml of the fish sauce, the sugar, and salt in a 3 quart/5¼-pint/3-l soup pot or Dutch oven. Bring to a boil. Reduce the heat and simmer.

3. Meanwhile, heat the oil in a frying pan. Add the shallots and garlic and stir-fry until aromatic. Add the crabmeat, the remaining 2 tsp/10ml fish sauce, and black pepper to taste.

3. Stir-fry over high heat for 1 minute. Set aside.

4. Bring the soup to a boil. Add the cornstarch mixture and stir gently until the soup thickens and is clear. While the soup is actively boiling, add the egg and stir gently.

5. Continue to stir for about 1 minute. Add the crabmeat mixture and asparagus with its canning liquid; cook gently until heated through.

6. Transfer the soup to a heated tureen. Sprinkle with the coriander, green onion (scallion), and freshly ground black pepper.

Asparagus and Crabmeat Soup (Mang Tay Nau Cua)

Ingredients

4 cups/1¾ pints/1 l chicken broth

1 tbsp plus 2 tsp/25ml nuoc mam (Vietnamese fish sauce)

½ tsp/2.5g sugar, ¼ tsp/1.25g salt

1 tbsp/15ml vegetable oil

6 shallots, chopped, 2 garlic cloves, chopped

1 cup/8oz/250g crabmeat

freshly ground black pepper

2 tbsp/30g cornstarch or arrowroot, mixed with 2 tbsp/30ml cold water

1 egg, lightly beaten

15oz/425g white asparagus spears, cut into 2 ½cm/1in sections with canning liquid reserved

1 tbsp/15g coriander (cilantro) leaves, shredded

1 green onion (scallion), thinly sliced

Method

1. Mix the dressing ingredients. Combine salad vegetables in a bowl, excepting the lettuce and cucumber, pour the dressing over them, cover, and refrigerate for 1 hour. Transfer to salad bowl.

2. Add chicken, lettuce, and cucumber. Toss together and sprinkle with mint and chili pepper rings.

Ingredients

2 cups/1 lb/450g cooked chicken, chopped

1 onion, finely sliced

1 carrot, cut in julienne strips

1 radish, finely sliced

1 stick celery, finely sliced

½ green or red bell pepper, seeded and finely sliced

1 cup/4oz/125g lettuce leaves, torn

¼ long cucumber, sliced diagonally

Chicken Salad

Dressing

5 tbsp/75ml lemon juice

⅓ cup/3½ fl oz/100ml water

3 tbsp/45g sugar

Garnish

1 tbsp/15g mint, chopped

1 small seeded red chili pepper, sliced

Method

1. Remove head, fins, and tail from fish and cut into 8—10 large pieces.
Combine fish, nuoc mam, pepper, and green onion (scallion), allow to marinate
for 15 minutes.

2. Place water in a large saucepan and bring to the boil. Add the fish with its juices
and the lemongrass. Reduce heat and simmer for 20 minutes.

3. Meanwhile, combine tamarind pulp and boiling water, and allow to soak
for 15 minutes. Strain mixture through a fine sieve and discard pulp.

4. Add the tamarind liquid, sugar, bamboo shoots, pineapple, and tomatoes
to the pan. Simmer for 4—5 minutes until fish is tender.

5. Divide beansprouts between serving bowls and spoon over hot soup.
Sprinkle over fresh herbs and deep fried shallots. Serve with lime
wedges and sliced chili pepper on the side.

Hot-and-Sour Fish Soup

Ingredients

2½lb/1kg firm-fleshed white fish (e.g. red
snapper)

1½ tbsp/20ml nuoc mam (fish sauce)

¼ tsp/1.25g white pepper

1 green onion (scallion), chopped

6 cups/1pint 8fl oz/1½ l water

2 stalks lemongrass, cut into 2in/5cm lengths
and crushed lightly

2oz/55g tamarind pulp

¼ cup/2fl oz/50ml boiling water

1 tbsp/15g sugar

¾ cup/6oz/175g sliced bamboo shoots

1 cup/8oz/250g sliced pineapple

2 tomatoes, cut into wedges

1 cup/8oz/250g bean sprouts

mixed Vietnamese herbs (coriander, bitter herb,
Asian basil)

deep fried shallots

lime wedges, sliced chili pepper

Method

1. Blanch cabbage leaves in boiling water and cut away any tough sections from the base.

2. Cut white ends from green onions (scallions) and finely chop four white heads. Slice two lengthwise for garnish. Slice green stalks into strips.

3. Mix chopped green onions (scallions) and 2 tbsp of the coriander with pork and shrimp. Season with pepper.

4. Into each cabbage leaf, place 1 tbsp/15g of mixture. First fold the leaf base then outer edges over it, and roll up. Carefully tie up each roll with a length of green onion (scallion) then place the packages gently into boiling broth and cook for 6 minutes.

5. Lift parcels into bowls, pour a cup of broth over each and garnish with remaining sliced green onions (scallions) and coriander. Dip rolls into fish sauce when eating.

Ingredients

1 cup pork, minced

½ cup prawns, minced

6 green onions (scallions)

4 tbsp/60g coriander, finely chopped

24 cabbage leaves

6¼cups/2½ pints/1.6 l chicken or pork broth

2½ tbsp/40ml fish sauce

Cabbage Packages in Soup

Method

1. Peel melon, remove seeds, cut into small cubes and purée in a liquidizer or food processor. Keep cool. Slice ginger finely and boil half of it in water with half the sugar until dissolved. Reduce the heat, add noodles, and simmer for 5 minutes. Remove, allow to cool, pour into bowl. Discard ginger and chili pepper.

2. In a saucepan, boil together remaining sugar and ginger and lime or lemon juice. Simmer until thick. Take from stove, cool, and discard ginger. Chill.

3. In individual bowls, set in larger ice-filled bowls, pour equal quantities of gingered melon purée. Top with noodles then the lime or lemon. Garnish each with a mint leaf. Serve each with two ginger cookies.

Ginger Melon Soup

Ingredients

1 small melon (about 1 lb 10oz/750g)

3½ cups/1¼ pints/800ml water

11oz/315g glass noodles

2oz/55g ginger, peeled

3½ oz/100g sugar

juice of 2 limes or lemons

2 ginger cookies

Method

1. Pour the water into a large pot. Add the shin bones and beef. Bring to the boil and skim the surface. Turn heat to medium-low, partially cover and simmer for two hours, skimming often, before add in remaining broth ingredients. Simmer another 90 minutes and remove from heat. Leave to cool.

2. Strain the broth through a fine sieve and discard bones, carrots, onion, and spices. Skim fat from broth. Cut the beef finely across the grain to paper thinness. Reserve.

3. Soak rice noodles in warm water about 20 minutes until soft, drain and reserve.

4. Return broth pot to heat to boil with fish sauce then reduce heat to very low. Fill a separate big pot three-quarters full of water and boil, add noodles and rinsed bean sprouts. Continue cooking until noodles are tender but not mushy. Bean sprouts should retain some crispness.

5. Serve boiling broth first then drained noodles into 6 bowls, top equally with beef, raw onion rings, chopped green onions (scallions), and thin raw steak slices, which will par-cook in the bowls, and garnish with coriander and mint leaves.

Tip

The beef will be easiest to slice if semi-frozen in the freezer.

Diners help themselves to chili rings and lime wedges. This recipe can also be adapted for chicken which takes less time to cook.

Ingredients

Broth

2¼ lb/1kg shin beef bones

12oz/340g lean stewing beef

12 cups/5¼ pints/3l water

1 large brown, unpeeled onion, halved

3 medium pieces unpeeled ginger, sliced

pinch of salt

1 cinnamon stick

6 whole cloves

6 peppercorns

6 coriander seeds

4 whole star anise

2 un-peeled carrots, cut into chunks

Additions:

8oz/225g thick steak in one piece

8oz/225g rice noodles

1lb/455g flat, thick, dried noodles

Beef Pho

2 tbsp fish sauce (nuoc mam)

1 brown onion, thinly sliced

3 green onions (scallions), finely chopped

½ cup/4oz/125g beansprouts

½ cup/2oz/50g fresh coriander (cilantro), torn into sprigs

½ cup/2oz/50g vietnamese mint leaves, chopped

1 small red chili pepper, seeded and sliced into rings

2 limes cut into wedges

Vietnamese

Method

1. Chop tomatoes into wedges. Cut fish into large bite-sized chunks. Heat the broth and add the fish. Reduce the heat and simmer for 6 minutes. Skim the surface, and add tomatoes, dried dill, and salt and pepper to taste.

2. Simmer a little longer until fish is cooked but not breaking up. Serve in a large bowl or individual bowls and garnish with fresh dill.

Ingredients

6 cups/1 pint 8 fl oz/1½ l chicken broth

1½ lb/750g fresh water fish fillets

3 medium tomatoes

salt and pepper

2 tbsp/50g chopped fresh dill

extra fresh dill

Fish Soup with Tomato and Dill

Vietnamese

Method

1. Finely julienne the papaya and toss with the finely julienned (sliced) green onions (scallions), white radish, chopped fresh herbs, and garlic.

2. To make the dressing, dilute the shrimp paste in 2 tbsp/50ml boiling water, then whisk with all other dressing ingredients. If the sauce is a little too acidic, add a little extra water as required to dilute the flavor to your taste. Continue whisking until the dressing is well mixed.

3. Toss the papaya-and-vegetable mixture in the dressing.

4. Pile on a plate and sprinkle with peanuts or dried shrimp.

Ingredients

26oz/750g green papaya

4 green onions (scallions), very finely julienned (sliced)

½ white radish (daikon or mooli), very finely julienned (sliced)

12 leaves Asian mint

12 leaves Thai or Italian basil

¼ bunch coriander (cilantro), leaves only (about 2oz/50g)

1 garlic clove, minced

2 tbsp/50g dried shrimp or crushed peanuts

extra Asian mint and basil leaves, to garnish

Green Papaya Salad

Dressing

¼ tsp/2.5g shrimp paste

2 tbsp/50ml boiling water

3 tbsp/45ml rice vinegar

3 tbsp/45ml lime juice

2 tbsp/30ml fish sauce

2 tbsp/50g sugar

1 tbsp/25ml sweet chili sauce

Method

1. Soak mushrooms for 30 minutes, drain, remove stalks, discard them, and chop the remainder.

2. Thinly peel cucumbers and cut into ½ in/1cm pieces. Scrape flesh out and discard. Parboil cucumber shells for 1 minute. Rinse in cold water, drain, and dust inside with a little of the cornstarch.

3. Drain water chestnuts, discard liquid, mash, and add rice flour, a dash of sesame oil and ¼ tsp/1.25ml each of sugar and salt. Add carrot and mushrooms and mix well. Stuff cucumber circles and place on a plate to steam, covered, for 15 minutes.

4. In a separate saucepan, mix a dash of oil with pepper to taste and ¼ tsp/1.25ml each of the remaining sugar and salt. Add remaining cornstarch. Stir in broth or water until smooth. Heat until thickened and pour over the cooked cucumber pieces.

Ingredients

1lb/500g cucumber

1½ cups/12oz/375g canned water chestnuts

4 dried black mushrooms

4 tbsp/60g cooked, diced carrot

2½ tbsp/60g glutinous rice flour

Steamed Stuffed Cucumbers

sesame oil

½ tsp/2.5g salt

½ tsp/2.5g sugar

pepper

1½ tsp/15g cornstarch

¾ cup/6fl oz/175ml broth or water

Method

1. Add pepper, garlic, fish sauce, and sugar to seafood. Pound or blend until combined. Pour into a bowl, cover with plastic wrap, and refrigerator for at least two hours, for flavors to mingle.

2. Oil hands, divide seafood paste into 8 portions and mold each smoothly around a sugar cane skewer.

3. Broil or barbecue over medium heat until golden and crisp or bake in a moderate (350°F/180°C oven) for 15–20 minutes. Arrange on serving plates with lettuce, mint, and coriander leaves, slices of chili, and lime slices, attractively arranged. Serve with Sweet and Sour Sauce.

Seafood Sugar Cane Skewers

Ingredients

1½ cups/12oz/350g shrimp or crabmeat, minced

1 garlic clove, crushed

black pepper to taste

½ tsp/2.5ml fish sauce

1½ tsp/7.5g sugar

8 sticks sugar cane, 4in/10cm long

1½ tbsp/40ml vegetable oil

garnish:

1 seeded finely sliced red chili pepper

1 lime, sliced into 8 wedges

mint

coriander and lettuce leaves

1 cup/8fl oz/250ml sweet-and sour-sauce

Method

1. Soak mushrooms in hot water for 40 minutes. Squeeze out liquid, remove stems, and chop the tops very finely. Place mushrooms and green onions (scallions) and pork in a bowl. Add fish sauce, eggs, salt, and pepper to taste and combine thoroughly.

2. Grease a loaf pan, add meat mixture, patting down firmly. Cover with foil, sealing well. In a larger roasting pan, pour hot water to half way up the loaf pan and place in moderately hot oven 400°F/200°C for about 60 minutes or until done. Test with knife or skewer which should come out cleanly from the center.

3. Allow the loaf to cool a little, run knife around the pan sides then unmold.

Slice and garnish with coriander (cilantro) leaves.

Baked Pork Loaf

Ingredients

12 dried mushrooms	2 tbsp/50ml fish sauce (nuoc mam)
2lb/1kg minced pork	pinch of salt
8 green onions (scallions), finely chopped	ground black pepper
5 eggs, beaten	coriander (cilantro) leaves, to garnish

Method

1. First, beat the rice vinegar and sugar together, and pour the mixture over the finely sliced onion rings. Allow to marinate for 1 hour, tossing frequently.

2. Cook noodles according to package directions (usually, rice noodles need only to soak in boiling water for 5 minutes, otherwise, boil for 1–2 minutes then drain immediately, and rinse under cold water).

3. Cut off the tough stalk of the asparagus, and cut the remaining stalks into 2cm/¾ in lengths. Simmer the asparagus in salted water for 2 minutes until bright green and crisp-tender. Rinse in cold water to refresh.

4. Toss the noodles with the reserved onion-and-vinegar mixture while still warm, then, using kitchen scissors, cut the noodles into manageable lengths.

5. To the noodles, add the cooked asparagus, chopped mint, coriander, cucumber, green onions (scallions), tomatoes, and roasted peanuts and toss thoroughly.

6. Whisk the lime juice, fish sauce, oil, and chili flakes together and drizzle over the noodle salad. Serve at room temperature.

Ingredients

3 tbsp/45ml rice vinegar

1 tbsp/15g sugar

1 small Spanish onion, finely sliced

9oz/255g dried rice noodles

2 bunches of asparagus

⅓ cup/3½oz/100g chopped fresh mint

⅓ cup/3½oz/100g chopped fresh coriander

1 small cucumber, peeled, seeded and thinly sliced

Herbed Rice Noodles
with Asparagus and Peanuts

6 green onions (scallions), finely sliced

3 beefsteak tomatoes, finely diced

¾ cup/6oz/175g roasted peanuts, lightly crushed

juice of 2 limes

2 tsp/20ml fish sauce

2 tsp/20ml olive oil

½ tsp/1.25g chili flakes

Vietnamese

Method

1. Cube beef. Add onion, garlic, ginger, chili peppers, curry powder, turmeric, pepper and 1 tsp salt. Toss to mix and cover with plastic wrap to marinate overnight, turning occasionally.

2. In a big, heavy-based saucepan, heat oil on high, add beef, turning to seal in flavors before pouring in the water, ½ tsp/2.5g salt, and fish sauce. After boiling, cover with lid, reduce heat, and simmer for about 1 hour, or until meat is cooked then add sugar and carrots until they are done, about 15 minutes.

3. Add cornstarch to coconut milk, stirring to dissolve. Pour this into the curry, stirring for 10 to 15 minutes until thickened. Serve in a casserole with rice and salad and coriander leaf garnish.

Beef Curry

Ingredients

2lb/1kg stewing beef	1 tbsp/15g sugar
1 large onion, sliced	1½ tsp/7.5g salt
4 garlic cloves, crushed	⅓ cup/3½fl oz/100ml vegetable oil
2 tbsp/30g ginger, crushed	1 cup/8fl oz/250ml water
2 red chili peppers, seeded and finely chopped	4½ tbsp/70ml fish sauce
3½ tbsp/100g hot curry powder	3 large carrots, chopped
2 tsp/10g turmeric	3 tbsp/45g cornstarch
1 tsp black ground pepper	2½ cups/1 pint/1.25 l coconut milk

Method

1. Soak mushrooms in hot water for 40 minutes. Remove stalks and discard.
Cut green onions (scallions) into 1½in/3½cm pieces. Seed green pepper and chili
and cut into pieces. Combine marinade ingredients.

2. Cut spare ribs into large bite-sized pieces and marinate 30 minutes. Deep-fry until
brown. Remove from heat. Sauté green onions (scallions) and mushrooms in oil,
return ribs to pan with ½ tsp/2.5g salt, sugar, dark soy sauce, ⅓ cup/3½ fl oz/100ml
water and stir fry. Add bell pepper, chili, and combined sauce ingredients.

3. Mix well, stirring, until the chili pepper just starts to lose its crispness.
Serve on a pre-heated heavy-metal grill pan so meat sizzles. Serve garnished
with mint sprigs.

Sizzling Spare Ribs

Ingredients

1lb/450g pork or beef spare ribs

8 dried mushrooms, 2 green onions (scallions)

1 green bell pepper, 1 red chili

½ tsp/2.5g salt, ½ tsp/2.5g sugar

1 tsp/5ml dark soy

⅓ cup/3½fl oz/100ml water, oil for frying

Marinade

½ tsp/2.5g salt, ½ tsp/2.5ml dry sherry

1 tbsp/15ml light soy sauce

2 tsp/10g cornstarch

Sauce

½ tsp/2.5g cornstarch, dash of sesame oil

ground black pepper, 1½ tbsp/20ml fish sauce,

mint leaves for garnish

Vietnamese

Method

1. Clean the crab well. Heat oil in a large saucepan. Stir-fry garlic, onion, lemongrass, and chili pepper over high heat for a few minutes.

2. Pour fish sauce, lime juice, and water into the pan, bring to the boil. Carefully place crab in saucepan. Cover with a tight-fitting lid. Cook over a medium high heat for 10–15 minutes, or until the crab is cooked.

3. Place crab on a serving platter. Add green onions (scallions) to the pan, reduce cooking liquid to about ¼ cup/2fl oz/50ml, and pour this over the crab.

4. Arrange bean sprouts over the hot crab, sprinkle liberally with deep fried shallots, and serve with extra lime juice and fish sauce.

Chili Crab with Lemongrass

Ingredients

1 large crab (1.5kg) or 2 smaller crabs

1 tbsp/15ml oil

2 garlic cloves, minced

1 onion, sliced

1 stalk lemongrass, finely sliced

4 chili peppers, sliced

2 tbsp/30ml fish sauce

2 tbsp/30ml lime juice

½ cup/4fl oz/125ml water

4 green onions (scallions), cut into 1in/2.5cm pieces

½ cup/4oz/125g beansprouts

deep fried shallots

Method

1. Slice steak into thin strips about 2in/5cm long. Separate cauliflower into flowerets then divide into two. Drain liquid from mushrooms, measure ½ cup/4fl oz/125ml and mix with cornstarch, 1 tbsp fish sauce, and oyster sauce. Peel and finely chop garlic. Cut onion lengthwise into eighths.

2. Pour 1 tbsp/15ml fish sauce over sliced meat and grind pepper over it. Turn and leave to stand for 20 minutes.

3. Heat the oil in a frying pan, add garlic and onion, and stir-fry until onion separates and softens. Add cauliflower and mushrooms. Cover, reduce heat, and cook for 4 minutes. Add meat and cook until meat is cooked to your liking. Stir in liquid mixture. Continue stirring till sauce thickens. On serving plate and garnish with coriander sprigs.

Ingredients

1 cup/7oz/200g fresh button mushrooms, whole

1½ tsp/7.5g cornstarch

½ cup/4fl oz/125ml water or broth

2 tbsp/50ml fish sauce

1 tsp/5g sugar

1 tsp/5ml oyster sauce

Beef, Cauliflower,
and Mushroom Stir-fry

8oz/225g steak

¼ cauliflower

vegetable oil

3 garlic cloves

1 medium onion

black pepper, ground

coriander sprigs, to garnish

Method

1. Heat oil in pan, add fish, and fry lightly until just brown. Transfer fish to a clay pot or stove-top casserole. Brown pork in pan and add to fish pot or casserole with garlic, broth, sugar, and chili peppers. Stir to combine, cover, and cook on medium heat until sauce is thickened.

2. In pan, sauté onion slices until tender. Add fish sauce to pot, stir and when pork and fish are cooked, place onions on top of mixture then fresh tomato, before serving dish at the table.

Claypot Fish

Ingredients

13oz/370g freshwater fish fillet,

cut into bite-sized pieces

oil for frying

1 cup/8fl oz/250ml chicken broth

4 oz/115g pork loin, sliced

10 garlic cloves, finely chopped

½ cup/4oz/125g sugar

2 seeded chili peppers, finely chopped

1 tbsp/15ml fish sauce

1 medium onion, sliced

1 medium tomato, sliced

Method

1. In a heavy-based pan, heat oil, add pork cubes, and turn until brown. Add garlic and onion and cook until the slices separate into rings and are transparent. Remove from heat.

2. In a separate saucepan, mix sugar with water and stir over low heat until sugar dissolves. Bring to boil then reduce heat and simmer, still stirring, until liquid is golden. Take pot off heat and carefully add fish sauce and lime juice which will spatter. Return to heat, stirring quickly to remove any lumps and until the sauce reduces a little.

3. Quickly return pork, garlic, and onions to reheat, add chili spice then caramel. Cook for 1 minute, stirring until combined. Transfer to serving dish and sprinkle green onions (scallions) on top.

Tip

Pour boiling water immediately into pot in which caramel has cooked or the caramel will stick fast and be very difficult to remove.

Ingredients

1½ lb/750g pork, cubed

2 medium onions, sliced

⅓ cup/3½ oz/100g sugar

¾ cup/6fl oz/175ml water

1½ tbsp/20ml fish sauce

1½ tbsp/20ml lime juice

½ tsp/2.5g salt

Caramelized Pork

1 seeded red chili pepper, sliced and chopped

½ tsp/2.5g five spice powder

2 garlic cloves, minced

oil for frying

2 green onions (scallions), chopped, for garnish

Vietnamese

Method

1. Angle-cut calamari into square pieces, open up with knife, and score each piece with a criss-cross pattern. Dry calamari pieces.

2. Make smooth batter of flour, cornstarch, and custard powder (used to provide color) with water. If using egg for color, add a little more flour, as mixture should not be too liquid.

3. Mix batter with calamari and cover for a few minutes. Heat oil in wok or frying pan until hot, add calamari and cook for about 3 minutes then remove calamari and drain away almost all oil. In the remaining oil, sauté onion and garlic until just tender. Stir in parsley or coriander and cook for 30 seconds. Return calamari to pan and sprinkle with a mixture of sugar, salt, pepper, and five-spice powder. Gently stir to combine.

4. Toss vermicelli into hot oil for near-instant crispy noodles and arrange them in a serving platter. Place calamari on top, sprinkle with a few drops of sherry (optional) and garnish with parsley or coriander sprigs.

Salt and Pepper Calamari

Ingredients

1lb/500g calamari, cleaned

small onion cut into little pieces

1 garlic clove, crushed

2 tbsp/50g chopped fresh parsley or coriander

vegetable oil for deep frying

1 tsp/5g sugar, ½ tsp/2.5g salt

1½ tsp/7.5g ground white pepper

½ tsp/2.5g five-spice powder

3 tbsp/45g self-rising flour

1 tbsp/15g cornstarch

1 tbsp/15g custard powder or 1 egg

4 tbsp/60ml cold water

4oz/125g rice vermicelli (cellophane) noodles

1 tbsp/125ml dry sherry (optional)

Method

1. Between two sheets of plastic film, pound chicken till thin. Slice into thin strips. Season with garlic, salt and plenty of pepper. Stir and leave for 10 minutes.

2. Heat pan, add 2 tbsp oil and sauté chicken quickly. Remove from pan. Reheat pan, add remaining oil, and sauté onion until it turns color. Add cauliflower flowerets and chili pepper and sauté for 10 to 15 minutes.

3. Mix cornstarch with vinegar and sauces until smooth. Add this to the broth.

4. Combine chicken with vegetables, add sauce, stir as the mixture thickens, and serve with steamed rice or noodles.

Ingredients

2 large chicken fillets

2 garlic cloves, minced

2 large onions, each cut into 8

2 cups/8oz/250g small cauliflower flowerets

1 red chili pepper, seeded and chopped

salt & ground black pepper to taste

4 tbsp/60ml vegetable oil

Sauce

2 tbsp/30g cornstarch

1 cup broth (powdered or cube will do)

1 tbsp/15ml soy sauce

1 tbsp/15ml vinegar

1 tbsp/15ml fish sauce

Chicken with Cauliflower

Tip

Thin rare beef strips can be used instead of chicken.

Method

1. Soak noodles in boiling water for 10 minutes. Chop into ¾ in/2cm sections. Soak mushrooms in boiling water for 10 minutes, drain, and slice. Soften garlic in oil over medium heat. Pre-heat oven to 300°F/150°C.

2. In a bowl, beat eggs, and add drained garlic, chicken,noodles, mushrooms, sugar, coriander, and salt and pepper to taste. Combine thoroughly and pour into lightly greased heatproof individual soup bowls or one large tureen.

3. Place bowls in a baking dish and fill it half-way with water. Cover the bowls and steam until cakes are set, about 30 minutes. Remove lids for just long enough to turn the top golden. Serve garnished with green onions (scallions) and a sprig each of coriander. Serve with separate bowls of nuoc mam and soy sauce for dipping.

Ingredients

2oz/55g cellophane noodles

4 dried mushrooms

2 garlic cloves, minced

2 tsp/10g fresh coriander (cilantro), finely chopped

1 tbsp/15ml vegetable oil

6 eggs

14oz/400g chicken fillet, minced

pinch of salt

ground black pepper

11/2 tsp/7.5g sugar

Chicken Egg Cakes

Garnish

1 green onion (scallion), sliced

6 sprigs coriander

nuoc mam, and soy sauce

Tip

Minced pork, beef, shrimp, or crabmeat can be used instead of chicken.

Method

1. Beat the eggs in a bowl, stir in beansprouts, green onions (scallions), and crabmeat, and add salt and pepper to taste.

2. Add oil to a frying pan to cover the base, heat it, and drop in all of the crab mixture, 1 heaping tbsp/20g at a time.

3. Fry until golden-brown on one side, then turn and brown the other side.

4. Remove from pan, and keep warm.

5. To make the sauce, blend together the cornstarch and sugar in a pan, add soy sauce, chicken broth, and fish sauce.

6. Slowly bring to the boil over a low heat, stirring all the time. Cook for 3 minutes (or until sauce is thickened). Stir the sherry into the mixture before serving.

Ingredients

3 eggs

1 cup/8oz/250g bean sprouts

3 green onions (scallions), chopped

1¾ cups/14oz/400g crabmeat

salt and cracked black peppercorns

oil (for deep frying)

Crabmeat Fritters

Sauce

2 tsp/10g cornstarch

1 tbsp/15g sugar

3 tbsp/45ml soy sauce

1 cup/8fl oz/225ml chicken broth

1 tbsp/15ml fish sauce

2 tbsp/30ml dry sherry

Method

1. Prepare vegetables. Remove outer leaves and tough tops and trim ends
of lemongrass and slice as finely as possible. Trim the beans and peel carrots.
Cut both vegetables diagonally into 1½in/3½cm pieces. Slice eggplant into
1in/2.5cm rounds, salt, let stand 10 minutes. Drain liquid and quarter each round.

2. Heat oil in a heavy-based pan, add green onions (scallions) and garlic, and sauté
until just golden. Add curry powder, shrimp paste if desired, lemongrass, and chili
peppers, and cook about 6 minutes. Add broth, coconut milk, fish sauce, and lime
leaves or citrus peel. Cover and bring to boil.

3. Reduce heat to medium, add carrots, potatoes, beans, and eggplant. Partially
cover and simmer until vegetables are tender and liquid has reduced.

Ingredients

2 green onions (scallions), sliced thinly

3 garlic cloves, crushed

2½ tbsp/75ml vegetable oil

2 stalks lemongrass

3 tbsp45g curry powder

2 tsp/5g shrimp paste (optional)

2 dried red chili peppers, chopped

1 cup/8fl oz/250ml coconut milk

1 cup/8fl oz/250ml broth

Curried Vegetables

1 tbsp/15ml fish sauce

2 lime leaves or strips of lime or lemon peel

½ cup/4oz/115g carrots

½ cup/4oz/115g green beans

1 cup/9oz/255g new potatoes, peeled and quartered

1 eggplant

salt

Method

1. Mix marinade ingredients, coat both sides of duck pieces and marinate, preferably overnight.

2. Put some oil in pan, place duck pieces in it with the marinade and cook till golden. Turn pieces and baste. Reduce the heat a little.When duck is almost cooked, sprinkle half the sugar on the pieces. Cook for 15 minutes then turn it again and sprinkle with the rest of the sugar. While sugar is caramelizing, add the orange juice and stir. Remove the pieces duck from the pan and reserve.

3. Peel the whole oranges, divide into segments, and arrange on serving plate. Add the duck. Stir orange sauce until it has the desired thickness, pour it over duck pieces and decorate with julienned orange rind and extra chili peppers.

Spicy Orange Duck

Ingredients

	Marinade
4¼lb/2kg duck, cut into serving pieces	
2 small red chili peppers, seeded and sliced	3 tbsp/45ml fish sauce
3 tbsp/45g sugar	1 tbsp/15g peeled ginger, finely chopped
2 cups/16 fl oz/500ml orange juice	1 tbsp/15g seeded red chili pepper, finely
2 oranges, juice squeezed,	chopped
rind of 1 orange cut into julienne strips	salt and pepper
vegetable oil	1 tbsp/15ml vegetable oil

Method

1. Prepare dipping sauce by mixing shrimp paste, a little extra oil, fish sauce, and sugar. Boil and add more sugar if desired.

2. Season fish with salt and pepper and cut into 1in/2.5cm pieces. In a heavy-based pan, heat oil, add fish, turmeric, and ginger. Turn gently and just before fish is done, add green onions (scallions), dill, and peanuts. Arrange lettuce and mint on a bed of rice and serve with the fish. Serve with dipping sauce.

Ingredients

1lb/500g boneless fish fillets

4 tsp/40g grated turmeric

2 tbsp/30g shrimp paste

¼ cup/2 fl oz/50ml soy bean oil

¼ cup/2 fl oz/50ml peanut oil

½ cup/2 oz/50g fresh dill, chopped

4 green onions (scallions), chopped

Hanoi-Style Fried Fish

1 heaping tsp/15g ginger, grated

¼ cup/2 fl oz/50ml fish sauce

1 tbsp/15g sugar

2 tbsp/30g crushed peanuts

salt and pepper

lettuce, mint leaves and cooked rice, to serve

Vietnamese

Method

1. Peel the outer layers from the lemon grass stalks and finely chop the lower white bulbous parts, discarding the fibrous tops. Put the chicken cubes into a large bowl, add the lemongrass and sesame oil, and toss to coat the chicken. Cover and refrigerate for at least 2 hours, or overnight.

2. Heat a wok or large, heavy-based frying pan, then add the vegetable oil. Add the chicken with its marinade and stir-fry for 5 minutes or until the chicken meat is firm.

3. Add the red pepper, peanuts, fish sauce, soy sauce, sugar, and salt to taste. Stir-fry for another 5 minutes or until the chicken and pepper are cooked. Sprinkle with the green onions (scallions) just before serving.

Stir-fried Lemongrass Chicken

Ingredients

4 stalks lemon grass

18oz/500g skinless boneless chicken breasts,

cut into 1in/2½cm cubes

1 tsp/5ml sesame oil

2 tbsp/30ml vegetable oil

1 red bell pepper, deseeded and chopped

2 tbsp/30g roasted salted peanuts, roughly chopped

1 tbsp/15ml soy sauce

1 tbsp/15ml fish sauce

½ tbsp/2.5g sugar

salt

2 green onions (scallions), chopped

lemon juice

Method

1. Combine rice flour, coconut milk, 3 eggs, and salt to make a pancake batter. Heat a little oil in an 8in/20cm nonstick frying pan, add enough batter to coat the bottom. Make pancakes in the usual manner until all batter is used.

2. Blend ginger, garlic, soy, and white sauces. Add crabmeat, mushrooms, green onions (scallions), and beansprouts, and season to taste. Place 1 tbsp/15ml of the mixture on each pancake. Tuck in ends and roll up like a burrito, so mixture doesn't escape.

3. Carefully roll each pancake in seasoned flour then in remaining beaten egg. Deep fry until golden. Serve on lettuce leaves, sprinkled with chopped coriander, accompanied by fish sauce with finely sliced, seeded red chili pepper. As a variation, use thinly rolled puff pastry or filo dough instead of pancakes. Pancakes can also be filled and served without deep frying.

Ingredients

oil for frying

2 eggs

2oz/55g seasoned flour

extra oil for deep frying

Pancake batter

⅔ cup/3oz/85g rice flour

pinch salt

3 eggs, beaten

½ cup/4 fl oz/125ml coconut milk

Hué Stuffed Pancake

Pancake Filling

½ tbsp/7.5g peeled, chopped ginger

1 garlic clove chopped

1 tbsp/15ml soy sauce

½ cup/4fl oz/125ml white sauce

⅔ cup/5oz/145g crabmeat

⅔ cup/3oz/85g chopped mushrooms

4 tbsp/1oz/30g chopped green onions (scallions)

4 tbsp/1oz/30g beansprouts

salt and pepper

Vietnamese

Method

1. Soak the cellophane noodles in a bowlful of hot water to cover for 5–10 minutes (until tender), then drain immediately and rinse in cold water (to halt the cooking time). Cut noodles with scissors to a manageable length and toss with vinegar, fish sauce, crushed peanuts, and shrimp.

2. Mix fresh herbs together and set aside. Finely shred the cabbage leaves and slice the green onions (scallions) into fine julienne. In a large bowl, mix together the herbs, both types of cabbage leaves, green onions (scallions), noodle mixture, and grated carrot, tossing thoroughly.

3. Soak 1 rice wrapper at a time in warm water for 30 seconds and lay it on a flat surface. Place a little of the mixed vegetable and noodle filling on it. Roll up tightly, folding in the sides to enclose the filling. Continue until all ingredients are used.

4. To make the peanut sauce, heat the oil and sauté the garlic and chili pepper until softened (about 2 minutes), then add all remaining ingredients and whisk. Bring to the boil and simmer until thickened slightly (about 3 minutes).

5. To serve, slice each roll on the diagonal, then arrange one half over the other. Serve the dipping sauce separately. The wrappers can also be fried.

Vietnamese Herb Salad Rolls with Peanut Sauce

Ingredients

2oz/55g packet cellophane noodles	**Sauce**
3 tbsp rice vinegar, 1 tbsp fish sauce	2 tbsp peanut oil
4 tbsp roasted peanuts (crushed)	5 garlic cloves (minced)
12 large shrimp, cooked and finely chopped	½ small red chili pepper, chopped
20 Thai basil leaves, finely sliced	5 tbsp/75g peanut butter
10 Asian mint leaves, finely sliced	1½ tbsp/40ml tomato paste
¼cup fresh coriander, finely chopped	3 tbsp/45ml hoisin sauce
4 leaves Chinese Napa) cabbage (bok choy)	1 tsp/5g sugar
2 cabbage leaves, finely shredded	1 tsp/5ml fish sauce
5 green onions (scallions)	¾ cup/6fl oz/175ml water
12-16 rice paper wrappers	¼ cup/2oz/30g peanuts (crushed)

Method

1. Soak dried mushrooms in hot water for about 30 minutes till soft. Meanwhile, separate eggs into two bowls, whites in one, yolks in the other. Beat both, adding a little wine to the whites and yolks to make them more liquid.

2. Grease a frying pan with a little pork fat or oil. Add a piece of pork to flavor the grease over medium heat, move it around, then remove. Add egg whites with wine to pan and, when firm, remove and place on a plate. Add more fat or oil to the pan, then pour off excess oil and add beaten yolks .

3. Reduce the heat. When bubbles form on top of egg, turn off heat, and place omelet on another plate. Boil 2 cups/16 fl oz/500ml water, and add the banana leaf in to clean and soften. Strain and place leaf or moistened cheesecloth on a board.

4. Mix pork with sesame seeds, garlic, canned or fresh chili pepper, sugar, fish sauce, and pepper to taste. Trim the dried mushrooms and add them. Add the fresh mushrooms and pound the mixture. Heat quickly in pan.

5. Use a spatula to spread one quarter raw pork mixture over the yolk omelet on a work surface. Top with mushrooms. Add another layer each of pork and mushrooms, place an egg white circle on top then another pork layer. Roll flat with an oiled rolling pin. Add single sausage and trim. Gently roll and fill in roll end with pork.

Ingredients

2 duck eggs

½oz/15g dried wood ear mushrooms

½oz/15g field mushrooms

7in/17½cm hot spicy cooked sausage,

2 tbsp/30ml fish sauce

2 tbsp/30g sugar, pinch black pepper

2 finely chopped canned chili peppers

or deseeded fresh red chili peppers

2 garlic cloves, minced

7oz/200g ground pork

oil or pork fat for frying

1 tsp/5g sesame seeds

pinch of black pepper,

rice wine or dry sherry

2 cups/16 fl oz/500ml water

1 banana leaf or cheesecloth/string

garnish:

slices of cucumber, tomatoes,

par-boiled cauliflower flowerets

and fresh parsley sprigs

Madame Thu's Steamed Egg Roll

6. Place roll on banana leaf or cheesecloth, tuck in ends, bind with string to hold shape, and steam in a double boiler for about 17 minutes. Remove till cool then refrigerate until cold.

7. On a serving platter, arrange cucumbers in a half-moon shape around the circumference. Arrange halved, cored, and sliced tomato in front to resemble a heart shape. Remove leaf or cheesecloth from cold roll, slice in 1in/2.5cm thickness and arrange in center of the plate, topped with parsley sprigs.

Tip

These appetizers are intended for a Valentine's Day party. Serve with a fish dipping sauce (nuoc cham).

Vietnamese

Method

1. Boil pork fat to soften. Finely chop again.

Add sherry, salt, sugar, and pepper. Place in the sun or in a warm place to soften

further .

2. Meanwhile, reserve a pinch of chopped chili pepper for sauce. Add the remainder

to the calamari with parsley and green onions (scallions). Put fish sauce in a small

saucepan and heat until liquid has nearly evaporated. Add this and any crystals

to the calamari.

3. Separate the egg and lightly beat in individual bowls. Combine pork fat mix with

calamari and add enough egg white to bind. Oil hands to make flat cakes

of calamari to fry in wok or frying pan, turning in oil, adding more as necessary.

The cakes will expand. Remove calamari cakes. Wipe the wok or pan with kitchen

paper.Dip the cakes in egg yolk to give yellow color and fry again in fresh oil.

4. To the reserved chili pepper, add other sauce ingredients and combine well. Slowly

heat until sugar is dissolved.

5. Thinly slice lime and bell pepper. Halve rings and arrange in a circle on plate with

thin circles of cucumber. Add hot calamari cakes, pour the sauce over them,

and garnish with coriander sprigs.

Calamari Cha (Cakes)

Ingredients

1lb/500g squid, finely chopped

2 tsp/20g ground pepper

2 tbsp/30g pork fat, finely chopped

1 tbsp/15ml dry sherry

pinch salt

1 tsp/5g sugar

1 small seeded orange chili pepper, finely
chopped

2 tbsp/30g parsley, chopped

3 green onions (scallions), chopped

3 tsp/15ml fish sauce

1 egg

vegetable oil

Sauce

2 tsp/10ml fish sauce

2 tsp/10ml lime or lemon juice or vinegar

2 tsp/10g sugar

Garnish

1 lime

½ seeded red bell pepper

½ cucumber

coriander sprigs

Method

1. Part-freeze steak to make it easier to cut each piece into 2 thin slices, making four slices.Place steak on a plate and cut into four slices. Spread each with bell pepper, garlic, and 1 tbsp oil. Turn steak to marinate it, cover, and refrigerate for 45 minutes.

2. Pour 2½ tbsp/40ml oil into a heavy-based pan, ensuring the based is coated. Separate the noodles with hands. Heat oil to medium, add noodles and press them in and down with hands and spatula to fit the pan. Heat until noodles are golden and crisp. Cook until browned then leave it in the pan for about 15 minutes as it will break up.

3. Loosen edges and base of pancake gently. Place a large plate over the pan and quickly invert the pan to settle the pancake on the plate. Gently slide the pancake back into the pan, uncooked side down and continue cooking 5 to 10 minutes. Return pancake to plate in the same manner and keep warm in low oven.

4. In same pan, heat 2½ tbsp/40ml oil until smoking, add meat and bell pepper mix and sear quickly on both sides, not overcooking. Mix sugar, fish sauce, broth and cornstarch till smooth and add to steak. Turn meat to absorb flavors, remove it and stir sauce rapidly until thick, returning steak briefly to coat with sauce.

5. Serve steak and sauce on top of pancake and cut into 4 or 8 if presenting as an entree. Top with sauce and garnish with chopped green onions (scallions).

Ingredients

11oz/300g fillet steak

6 tbsp/90ml vegetable oil

½ red bell pepper, deseeded and sliced

3 tsp/15g garlic, minced

½ tsp/2.5g ground black pepper

Noodle Pancake with Garlic Beef

14oz/400g fresh, soft noodles

2 tsp/10g cornstarch

2 tsp/10g fish sauce

1 tbsp/15g sugar

½ cup beef broth

2 green onions (scallions) chopped

Vietnamese

Method

1. Heat oil in pan, add garlic and shrimp, stir-fryfor 2 minutes. Add onion, zucchini, and bell pepper, stirring for 2 more minutes. Remove from stove.

2. In another pan, heat curry paste for 1 minute, stirring constantly so it does not stick. Add coconut milk and bring to boil.

Mix cornstarch with water. Add sugar, fish sauce, and cornstarch to thicken.

Add shrimp with vegetables. Garnish with coriander leaves and serve with steamed rice.

Ingredients

12 cooked jumbo shrimp

2 garlic cloves, minced

1 cup/8fl oz/250ml coconut milk

1 onion, sliced

½ green bell pepper, seeded and sliced

2 tbsp/30ml vegetable oil

Shrimp Curry

1 medium zucchini, sliced

½ tbsp/7.5g green curry paste

1 tbsp/15ml fish sauce

1 tsp/5g sugar

1 tsp/5g cornstarch

1 tbsp/15ml water

Method

1. Shell, remove heads, and devein shrimp but retain tails. Finely chop three green onions (scallions). Cut the remaining two into thin strips 1in/2½cm long.

2. In a saucepan, heat sugar until golden, add 3 tbsp of the water, and stir until sugar dissolves. Boil, then simmer gently for about 3 minutes, until caramel darkens but doesn't burn. Add remaining water after removing pot from heat but take care it does not spatter. Reheat, stirring quickly to remove lumps.

2. Pour oil in heavy pan and, over medium heat, fry chopped green onion (scallion) and garlic. Add shrimp and cook for a few seconds until it turns pink. Slowly add fish sauce and warm caramel to the shrimp mixture. Combine and cook 1 minute before adding lime or lemon juice, salt, brown sugar, and sliced green onion (scallions). Stir together and serve topped with bell pepper strips.

Ingredients

1lb/455g raw shrimp

4 garlic cloves, finely chopped

5 green onions (scallions)

4½ tbsp/70g sugar

⅓ cup/3½ fl oz/100ml water

Shrimp in Caramel

oil for frying

1 tbsp/15ml lime or lemon juice

1 tbsp/15ml fish sauce

1 tbsp/15g brown sugar

pinch salt

⅓ green bell pepper, to garnish

Vietnamese

Method

1. Add a few drops of wine to pork fat, black pepper, sugar, and a little salt in a bowl. A Vietnamese will take the bowl into the sun to warm and melt the fat until it is transparent.

2. Chop shrimp very finely until mushy. Place in bowl. Add peppercorns and a littlesalt and pepper.

3. Fry onion until transparent, drain oil, and add onion to ground pork. Combine, add shrimps, pork fat, and dill or parsley and/or optional chili pepper with shrimp.

4. Crush bouillon cube finely and mix with bread crumbs. Work some oil into your hands, form walnut-sized balls, dip each in beaten egg and bread crumbs. Deep-fry in oil in a wok or pan until golden, quickly drain on kitchen paper and serve on a plate layered with lettuce.Top with coriander (cilantro) leaves and strips of finely peeled carrot.

Ingredients

1 cup/8oz/225g shelled shrimp

1 cup/8oz/225g ground pork

4 tbsp/2oz/55g pork fat, chopped

3 drops rice wine/dry sherry

1 tsp/5g sugar

2 tbsp/10g freshly milled black pepper

salt and black pepper to taste

1 small brown onion, finely chopped

1 egg, beaten

Shrimp Balls

2 tbsp/30g fresh chopped dill or parsley

vegetable oil for frying and handling

¼ cup/2 oz/30g breadcrumbs

1 chicken bouillon cube

seeded, small, red chili pepper, finely chopped (optional)

Garnish

lettuce leaves, fresh coriander leaves, and peeled carrot strips

Vietnamese

Method

1. Fry onion until tender in oil, drain and add to combination of ground meats, 1 egg, and cooked rice. Mix well. Add salt and pepper to taste. Form mixture into small balls.

2. Mix batter ingredients. Gently toss balls in seasoned flour in a bag, dip in batter, fry until golden, and drain. Reserve.

3. To make the sauce, fry onions until tender, add sherry, vinegar, sugar, broth, and pineapple juice. Cook for 6 minutes, add tomato paste and boil for 4 more minutes.

4. Process the pineapple, ginger, and garlic with a little water in a blender and add to the sauce with chili pepper powder. (Add more if desired.) Blend the arrowroot with more water until smooth and add to sauce. Stir until clear and thick, adding more water if too thick. Add meatballs to sauce to heat through before serving.

Sweet-and-Sour Meatballs

Ingredients	**Sauce**
1 cup 8oz/225g ground beef	2oz/55g onions, finely chopped
1 cup 8oz/225g ground pork	2 tbsp/50g sugar, 4 tbsp/60ml dry sherry
½ cup/4oz/115g rice, cooked	2 tbsp/30ml white vinegar (acetic acid)
1 cup/8oz/225g onions, finely chopped	1 cup/8 fl oz/250ml beef broth
1 egg, beaten	1 cup/8 fl oz/250ml pineapple juice
½ cup/2oz/55g flour seasoned with salt and pepper	4 tsp/20ml tomato paste
	¼ cup/2oz/55g chopped pineapple
oil for frying, extra salt and pepper	1 tsp/5g fresh ginger, chopped
	1 garlic clove, finely chopped
	pinch of chili powder, 1 tbsp/15g arrowroot,

Batter

1 egg

⅓ cup/3oz/85g all-purpose flour

⅔ cup/6½ fl oz/100ml water

Method

1. Soak about 25 bamboo skewers overnight in boiling water for at least 45 minutes so they will not burn when cooking. Combine marinade ingredients.

2. Cut chicken into thin strips and add to marinade, ensuring each strip is covered. Cover and refrigerate several hours or overnight.

3. Drain and reserve marinade for another use or discard. Thread chicken strips on to skewers. Barbecue or broil about 3 minutes until brown.

4. Serve as part of a main course or appetizers with nuoc cham (fish dipping sauce) or peanut sauce (see page 78).

Ingredients

2¼ lb/1 kg boneless chicken fillets

Marinade

2 green onions (scallions), chopped

1 stalk lemongrass, peeled and finely sliced

2½ tbsp/40g sugar

1 small, seeded red chili pepper, crushed

1 tbsp/15ml fish sauce (nuoc mam)

Spicy Chicken Skewers

1 tbsp/15ml soy sauce

1 tbsp/15ml peanut oil

1 tbsp/15ml coconut milk

1½ tsp/7.5g five-spice powder

Method

1. Trim stalks of water spinach (available from oriental grocery stores). Blanch spinach by plunging it into boiling water, then refresh it in cool or iced water. Drain completely.

2. Make peanut sauce in saucepan by combining all ingredients and stirring over low heat until smooth.

3. Fry green onions (scallions) and garlic until tender. Add peanuts to heat then spinach and peanut sauce. Garnish with coriander.

Ingredients

2 cups/8oz/500g water spinach or spinach

2 garlic cloves, crushed

3 green onions (scallions), sliced

¼ cup/2oz/50g peanuts, crushed

1½ tbsp/45ml vegetable oil

salt and pepper

Peanut Sauce

⅓ cup/3½ oz/100g smooth peanut butter

½ cup/4fl oz/125ml coconut milk

1½ tbsp sugar

⅓ cup/2½ fl oz/100ml sweet chili sauce

2 tsp/10ml lime or lemon juice

⅓ cup/3½ oz/100g chicken broth

Spinach with Peanut Sauce

Garnish

coriander springs

Method

1. In hot water, soak vermicelli for 5 minutes until soft. Drain, cut into 2in/5cm lengths and reserve.

2. Add 3 tbsp/45ml oil to the wok or pan. Add the garlic and chicken (or crab and pork) and cook about 8 minutes, mashing with a fork so they do not clump together. Add cabbage, carrot, green onions (scallions), and vermicelli to cook on high for about 3 minutes until vegetables soften.

3. Turn off heat, add salt, sugar, pepper, and oyster sauce. Stir to mix well. When mixture is cool, brush each side of the rice wrappers or dip them hot water to moisten them or they will dry and break. Place 1 tbsp of the mixture into each wrapper, turn sides in first, roll and seal each with beaten egg. Refrigerate until needed.

4. Heat extra oil in wok or pan. Deep fry rolls until golden. Serve on lettuce leaves garnished with lettuce and mint and serve with bottled sweet chili pepper sauce or fish dipping sauce.

Ingredients

20–25 rice paper wrappers

(some may be broken)

¾ cup/11oz/310g ground chicken (or half crabmeat, half ground pork)

⅔oz/20g green bean thread vermicelli

1 carrot, cut into thin strips

¼ cabbage, cut into fine strips

2 green onions (scallions), minced

1 tsp/5g sugar

½ tsp/2.5g salt

Spring Rolls

½ tsp/2.5 white pepper

1 tbsp/15ml oyster sauce

3 cloves garlic, minced

3 tbsp/45ml vegetable oil

extra oil for deep frying

1 egg, beaten

Garnish

lettuce and mint leaves

Method

1. Make the broth by boiling all the broth ingredients together then simmering for an hour. Strain reduced broth and discard the bones and big vegetables.

2. Boil chicken pieces in broth for 15 minutes, skimming the surface. Add vermicelli and softened dried wood ear mushrooms and cook until vermicelli is done.

3. Serve, season and sprinkle with chopped green onion (scallion).

Ingredients

1 cup/8oz/225g Chinese mung bean vermicelli

½ cup/125g/4oz dried wood ear mushrooms, trimmed and soaked

1 cup/8oz/250g chicken breast, cut into pieces

salt to taste

½ tsp/2.5g black or white pepper

2 tbsp/50g chopped green onions (scallions)

Vermicelli and Chicken Soup

Broth

8 cups/3½ pints/ 2l water

3 tsp/45ml fish sauce

1 onion, quartered

3lb/1½ kg pork bones

1lb/455g chicken wings, bones and/or leftover meat scraps

2 cups/1lb/455g of 2 of the following:whole carrot, quartered cauliflower, whole

green beans and/or quarter of a cabbage

Method

1. Cut tops from tomatoes, remove core and pulp, and set aside. Mash tofu and mix in a bowl with mushrooms, garlic, green onions (scallions), fish sauce, pepper, egg, and cornstarch. Fill tomatoes with the mixture.

2. In a large frying pan over high heat, pour in oil and carefully add tomatoes, stuffed side down. Cook about 4 minutes, turn to low and cook about 6 minutes.

3. Serve garnished with coriander and with Sweet-and-Sour Sauce.

Ingredients

6 firm, large tomatoes

½ cup firm tofu, drained

1 cup fresh mushrooms, chopped

3 garlic cloves, minced

4 green onions (scallions), chopped

1 tbsp fish sauce

Tofu-Stuffed Tomatoes

1 tsp/5g ground white pepper

1 tbsp/15g cornstarch

1 egg, beaten

¼ cup/2fl oz/50ml vegetable oil

Garnish

¼ cup/2oz/50g coriander, chopped

Vietnamese

Method

1. Soak mushrooms in boiling water for 30 minutes. Drain and discard stems. Slice.

2. Chop the hindquarter into chunks, using a cleaver to get through the bone. Pour boiling water over pieces to fatten skin, drain, dry with kitchen paper and, over medium heat, brown turkey in just enough oil to cover a heavy-based pan. Cook in batches, wiping pan clean with kitchen paper after each batch and adding more oil as necessary.

3. To the clean pan and fresh oil, return turkey, add soy sauce, sherry, sugar, mushrooms and peel from 1 orange and bring to boil.

4. Turn heat down to simmer, cover, and cook, stirring and skimming scum from surface occasionally until turkey is tender. Season with salt and pepper, remove from heat and stand covered for 5 minutes, discard orange peel and serve topped with sauce. Garnish with peel from remaining ½ orange and mint.

Ingredients

1 cup/4oz/125g dried mushrooms (ceps or wood ears)

3½lb/1½kg turkey hindquarter

2½ tsp/15ml vegetable oil

2 tbsp/30ml soy sauce

2 tbsp/30ml dry sherry

3 tsp/15g sugar

Turkey with Mushrooms

peel from 1½ oranges

salt and pepper to taste

garnish mint sprigs

Note

Chicken or duck can be used in this recipe.

Vietnamese

Method

1. Pre-heat oven to 325°F/170°C. Sift flour, sugar. baking soda, and salt into a bowl. Add ginger and cinnamon. Work butter in with hands until texture of bread crumbs. Beat golden syrup and egg together and gradually add to flour mix to form dough.

2. Form into small balls and place well apart on to greased cookie sheets to bake until crisply golden.

Ginger Cookies

Ingredients

1 cup/4oz/125g all-purpose flour

½ cup/4oz/125g superfine (caster) sugar

¼ tsp/2.5g baking soda

2 tbsp/30g ground ginger

pinch salt

1 tsp/5g ground cinnamon

2oz/60g butter

1 small egg

1 tbsp/15ml dark corn syrup or golden syrup

Method

1. To make the caramel, dissolve the sugar over low heat, in a small, heavy-based pan, swirling constantly until the sugar becomes golden. Stir in hot water carefully as the mixture will splatter. Quickly stir to dissolve any lumps and boil about 2 minutes until liquid and dark brown but not burned.

2. Grease a 6-cup/2½-pint/1.5 l soufflé dish with butter or margarine and pour the caramel into it. Tilt dish to ensure caramel coats the base.

3. To make the custard, beat eggs and vanilla in a large bowl. Combine coconut milk and milk with sugar in a saucepan and cook over low heat until sugar dissolves. Remove from stove and beat quickly into eggs and vanilla so eggs do not curdle. Sieve custard only if it is lumpy. Pour slowly into soufflé dish on top of caramel.

4. Pre-heat oven to 325°F/160°C In the base of a large roasting pan, place two layers of paper toweling, then the soufflé dish before pouring hot water into the roasting pan to come half-way up the soufflé dish. Bake in the center of the oven for about 50 minutes or until a knife inserted into custard is clean when removed. Do not allow water to boil. Remove soufflé dish. Cool in a pan of cold water. Chill, covered with plastic wrap, preferably overnight.

5. To serve, run a knife round the inside edge of the soufflé dish and place a dinner plate on top. In a quick movement, invert the dish and the crème caramel will unmold onto the plate. Serve alone or with whipped cream. Place a mint sprig in the center to garnish.

Ingredients

Caramel

¼ cup/2oz/50g sugar

¼ cup/2fl oz/50ml water

Custard

1 cup/8fl oz/250ml fresh, canned, or powdered reconstituted coconut milk

1 cup/8fl oz/250ml milk

Coconut Flan with Caramel
(Crème Caramel)

Vietnamese

¼ cup/2oz/50g sugar

4 eggs

1 tsp/5ml vanilla extract

Method

1. Mix together all dried ingredients. Add, while stirring, the boiling water, bring to boil, and simmer, still stirring for 10 minutes until thick. Stir in almond extract. Pour into lightly-greased serving bowl, cool, cover, and refrigerate.

2. Serve with a large bowl of cannedor fresh, peeled lychees, gooseberries, or fresh guava and cream if desired.

Ingredients

⅓ cup3oz/85g ground rice

⅔ cup/6oz/170g ground almonds

4 tbsp/2oz/55g powdered unflavored gelatin

⅔ cup/6oz/170g superfine (caster) sugar

4 tbsp/2oz/55g unsweetened shredded coconut

4½ cups/2 pints/1.25l boiling water

few drops of almond extract

Almond Rice Jello

Vietnamese

Method

1. Preheat the oven to 350°F/180°C and butter a 9in/22cm nonstick cake pan.

2. Crush the toasted macadamia nuts in a food processor and set aside.

3. Peel the mangoes and dice the flesh, saving as much juice as possible, then reserve some nice pieces of mango (about ⅓ cup /3oz/85g) and process the remaining mango flesh with all the reserved juice. You should have about 1 cup/8fl oz/250ml mango purée.

4. Beat the softened butter and vanilla extract with half the sugar and beat until thick and pale. While beating, add the remaining sugar, and beat until all the sugar has been added. Add the eggs, one at a time, beating well after each addition.

5. In a separate bowl, mix the crushed nuts, flour, and baking powder together.

6. Remove the bowl from the mixer and add the flour mixture, stirring well to combine. Add the mango purée and mix gently.

7. Spoon the batter into the prepared pan, then sprinkle the chopped macadamia nuts and reserved diced mango over the batter and swirl through.

8. Bake at 340°F/170°C for an hour, then remove the cake pan, from the oven and cool in the pan. When cool, remove the cake from the tin. Dredge with powdered sugar.

9. To prepare the cream, sprinkle the nutmeg over, whip the cream and nutmeg together, until the cream is thick and fragrant. Serve alongside the cake with some mango slices.

Mango Cake with Nutmeg Cream

Ingredients

1 cup/8oz/250g unsalted, roasted macadamia nuts

3 large mangoes, about 26oz/750g total weight

1 cup/9oz/255g butter

1 cup/8oz /250g superfine (caster) sugar

1 tsp/5ml vanilla extract

4 large eggs

2 cups/8oz/250g all-purpose flour

1½ tsp/7.5g baking powder

½ cup/2oz/50g toasted macadamia nuts, chopped

About powdered (icing) sugar

2 cups/16 fl oz/500ml heavy (double) cream

1 tsp/5g nutmeg

1 mango, sliced, for serving

Vietnamese

Index